Morphē Arts Publications, London UK.

Morphē Arts is an independent Christian charity who offer mentoring to recent graduates of the Creative Arts.

Words and photographs by Miriam Ettrick
Cover illustration and illuminations by Laura Sewall

Morphē
Arts

THE THINGS WE BURN

— MIRIAM ETTRICK —

INTRODUCTION—
BETWEEN THE SNOW-FLAKED ASHES

As a child, I remember sitting in the attic of a cabin in the woods, waiting for the rain. The air was hot and heavy, the farmers worried about drought and crops – there hadn't been rain for months. But as I sat on my small bed, I listened, against the faint rumble of thunder in the distance, to the wisest woman I know describing her darkest battle. In the midst of it she turned inward, pushing out of her life those who cared about her, until she was alone. She was a bush in the wasteland, she told me, there was poison in her roots, so that none would dare grow nearby.

One day, after years of living like this, she took a walk down to the creek at the edge of her property, where she wrote down her bitterness, those who had wronged her, even her own infant son. There she built a bonfire and watched the pages go up in smoke, the waters run black with soot and wash her clear.

Some years later, I found myself in an upstairs room of a stately home turned retreat centre, fire crackling in the hearth, trees blowing against the windows. The centre coordinator was explaining the exercise – writing out a list of people who we felt had hurt us. Furtively, we crouched over our papers, drawing people to mind, inscribing them onto our scraps of paper. One by one, we shuffled to the grand fireplace and released them to the flames, until the names were lost to ash and memory.

Months afterward, in a darkened chapel where tears had been shed, soft words spoken, a friend and I knelt below a sign that read "Please do not extinguish the light," around an ever-glowing candle. When there were no more words, we passed around the paper and pen. We wrote our pain in silence and silently held each leaf to the candleflame, watching them curl and crumble into the mottled carpet.

Back in the forest cabin, the heat broke and the rains came, in a single deluge. I peered out the attic window to see, in each lightning flash, the figures of my parents running back to the cabin, coat-collars raised over their heads, splashing through the paths. There would be no drought. The crops would grow again. That night, I fell asleep to the drumbeat of raindrops on the wooden roof above me, dreaming of old desert trees.

What can newness discover from burning
  when a charred stump is all that we've left?
When you were a desert shrub, a young fern
  calloused by salt, you stretched out roots in theft,

drove all away. That bush was burnt
  in slips of paper, names like leaves, scattered
descriptive hate, washed away in current
  streams, where you learnt to draw strength, undisturbed;

you're a tree stripped raw with crumbling moss,
  clustered with small shoots, bending to attend
the rustling regret of leaves, breathless
  cries from pinpoints of life that fear and

long for your fire-light, comfort in hope,
  immune to rivalries interred in smoke.

Immune to rivalries interred in smoke,
an old tree splits, shreds and falls with its charred

innards exposed and, crumbling from the stroke,
buds scatter, shining against white stripped bark.

The dissection is complete - your self-split
reveals life-lines etched in wood, inside

ridges marked with curves of carving, sits
an upright leaf, caught in branch and light.

The rest are tangle-separate. They appear
fallen, beautiful in devastation

where wind-blown shavings settle as snow tears,
displayed to the sun, a revelation

of weakness used anew, as returning
leaves flicker from the charcoal patterning.

3

Leaves flicker from the charcoal patterning.
The yawning sunrise, curtained high, parades
through shadows, rakes our vast cloyed river-spring.
Your last green leaf alights the barricade.

Ash-water blurs through debarred decay, caught
in thick impasto, your external swirl
crushed under quilted ripples, brought
to spine-edged seams, shafted out of pearl.

Infection blotches scar-maroon on leaves;
your abscessed branch distends with black balloons.
Below, projected outward, uneven
parallels fall, unknotted on grass dunes.

These shapes uncover the terrain we took
in crackling flax, and the bruised reeds we broke.

In crackling flax, and the bruised reeds we broke,
we built a barricade, a house for two,
where overgrown thickets replaced the oak
fence and an army of ponies accrued.

This is our landscape - this hill overlooks
all that we have - our boundary entwined
with wires, that melted slowly and twisted, cooked
by the sun into pastel outlines.
At base there's water, never the same, swept.

We bury ribbon-hearts here, in snow where
none will find them. The cold is nothing yet,
the frost, a new solid experience. There -
water and buds break through cracked shells, ones
we've harvested as chaff, as false intentions.

We've harvested the chaff, the false intentions.
and locked them in barns, safe from the embrace
of winds, unfair whispers of attention
from mice. Hidden daffodils find crevices
until all that remains are dead florets

and seasons of unsuccessful heather
that we'd hoped would spread in mottled blankets
to cover us, destroyed instead by weathered
storms. I find you in one of these, under
eaves dripping onto bent back, patiently
pressed against planks, soaking in blue jumper.

We tear down the barn. In disassembly
we create a shelter from the things we break;
all that we have, we promise to mistake.

All that we have, we promised to mistake,
as the friendship we had grew up and we
changed, as the world silenced our debates.

We separated the road at the pine-tree
edge of our land, moved halves and split in.
Under our roof, squirrel kittens are born
and we swap sides - you'll hold a kitten,
I'll tend a garden, wage war with thorns.

Some days, your wounded eyes appear among
my purple trampled crocuses, on bank, flattened,
and I collect you in a vase, or hung
to dry, watch you wilt, whatever happens.
In the hall, pine stalks burn as prevention,
the sacrifice to fuel our dissension.

7

The sacrifice that fuelled our dissension
bred in damp silences, over that cold
winter, in the attic, your attention
on branches around, whittling, as you holed

yourself up, your legs propped up in your chair,
numb and blotched. I forgot to bring you coffee
or crutches, or help you downstairs.
I polished kitchen floors; while you shaved trees.

I wheel you up the hill, one evening,
to find the thicket burnt, the ponies gone.
Above, crows continue their storm-cry, dark wings
over crumpled heather. You stoop to pick one.

Its tiny bells fragment in your hand, flake
and crumble, brittle-black, with every shake.

8

They crumble, brittle-black, with every shake, as they catch the flames,
   one by one by one – the wooden squirrel, pony, all those shapes you
   worked so hard to make in months, gone in instants. As I throw them in,
   you stare.

I lose myself searching through black furrows that evening, following
   caught horse-hair strands in wheel-tracks, startled showers of sparrows
   with rapid fire calls. The field roars. Alone, I choke in clouds – a dizzy
   breath, eyes water. With the stream as my guide, wind-blown, I find you,
   huddled across with ponies. I don't ask about scorched hair; you won't explain.

After the flames, always too late, comes rain.

After the flames, always too late, the rain
blurs through our vision - like our untried rage -
to darken the heavy land, mark out each stain.

We've made a fragile world - monochrome pages
unfurl into silk fields, bound by rooflines
and shadows, long as earth. From above,

our images puddled, reflect the times
when we learnt to honour, pretend in love
to hide the thunder of each waterfall.

We stand for hours in these forgotten fields
that our fires have deserted, and recall
aches deeper than reflections can reveal,

the landscapes in our memory where now,
between the snow-flaked ashes, green wheat grows.

 **10.**

Between the snow-flaked ashes, green wheat grows,
　　to form an ear-lapped path in thickening white.
Cold brushes back your hair, as you follow
　　this bend to the hill. Our uncertain light,
frozen in diamond to dew-point, now gleams -
　　a sharp reminder of regretted fires.

You've walked here before in dust-settled dreams
　　where tangled branches stiffen, hard coal wires
sketch, in pen-and-ink, the things we've lost.
　　You felt these weighted breaths, as you lay, unslept
re-walked the path barefoot, toes barbed with frost,
　　burning through footprints from promises kept.

The words we lost, with wisdom we'll retain
　　as silence pours into our fire-stroked plain.

As silence pours into our fire-stroked plain,
        we long for rain-songs of sea and sky to
encapsulate our symphony, contain
        all our uncertain voices. For now, you

incant my lament, cradle your disgrace
        as we look for confessions to reverse
the burden of forgiveness - to replace
        your guilt with something other than my hurt -

so that in time, by grace our storms have brought,
        this plain will once again swell up with noise.
We stand together (alone) with one thought
        look up, wait for the sea to fall from skies

until, filled with the grief of all we know,
        our mud-ridged interventions overflow.

Our mud-ridged interventions overflow
where, between the mud, we captured sky
in strips and burning tips of cloud, that glow
as each finds the same stretch of sunlit dye
or fade to hidden shades of deep grey smoke
which shift in eastern patterns swept across
by birds in engrained specks across the slopes.

This fire dies slowly, its embered exhaust
curls less but clumps around the source in wisps
stretching outward to thin threads. Before we
lose iridescence, before what exists
in gold sparks dissipates to glory,
we'll stand, and with a heavy heart proclaim
Later, in melting ash, we'll find the blame.

13

Later, in melting ash, we find the blame
that trickles down from the tree-tops, sets off
strings of bells through the fragile membranes
of star-grazed webs, amasses droplets, froth,
and punctures our barricade, now dwindled.

The treasury of ribbon-hearts exposed
in ashes and snow, collapses inward,
and spills in winter wind and warmth. We closed
off words and, expecting them to stay there,
built an alphabet from snowflakes. We smiled

through drifts in conversations, while aware
we cannot bury grief in something fragile.
The rain uncovers all - dread wrapped in pain
we fought to lose, and never thought to gain.

14

We fought to lose and never thought we'd find
a home - a porch in shades of paper-white
and a painted fence where, under our tree-lines,
fresh swirls of fledglings study paths of flight.

Around our boundary are thriving stocks
of heather blossom. We choose paint - eggshell
blue - for the gate to the new paddock,
find a forgotten kitten, tortoiseshell
and sooted black; we name her Cinders.

When watercolour shadows fade from doors,
and frost returns, knife-sharp, to our windows
we look across our burnt landscape once more
to mark the verdant shifts which come with spring.
What can newness discover from burning?

What can newness discover from burning?
  Immune to rivalries interred in smoke,
leaves flicker from the charcoal patterning,
  in crackling flax, and the bruised reeds we broke.

We've harvested as chaff the false intentions,
  all that we have, we promised to mistake,
the sacrifice to fuel our dissensions.
  They crumble, brittle-black, with every shake.

After the flames, always too late, comes rain.
  Between the snow-flaked ashes, green wheat grows,
as silence pours into our fire-stroked plain,
  our mud-ridged interventions overflow.

Later, in melting ash, we'll find the blame
  we fought to lose, and never thought we'd gain.

EPILOGUE—
WHERE THE GREEN WHEAT GROWS

There are echoes I find myself returning to, as I walk the fields beyond the city or the hidden copse at the end of my street, with my camera and notepad. For me, the work of a writer is that of an observer. I watch the seasons pass, the fields turn to gold and green to brown stubble and back again. Even now, as the winter draws in, they are ploughed, tilled smooth and seeded. From my seat on the hillside I can see the new wheat, impossibly green, hear the leaves and birdsong and children's voices blown on the wind.

Often, I walk down to the little white cottage with its eggshell paint, beside the busy road where trucks screech closer than comfort. It has stood empty for many years, the paint peeling from the gate, visible only through the mess of hedgerow. In the pony field across the road, a pale foal is born to a piebald mother. We watch him grow, his coat darkening from grey to black with age, his tail a tiny floppy rug. This week we arrived to find the field filled with building materials and emptied of ponies, moved on to winter pastures and warmer shelters.

The cottage has recently been bought, boarded up and fenced off. A glimpse of the yard shows the brushwood laid out for a pyre; the garden dug through with trenches. The new high slats cut out the light and the view from the roadside, so I can no longer stare through the tangled branches at the windows, imagining the lives within.

In the fields, the rain collects between mud tracks and the skies darken overhead. On the walk home I encounter, in the remains of a fire charred to newspaper ash, a gathering of wildflowers—a last memory of things burnt and lost and found.